BIKES
on the Move

Willow Clark

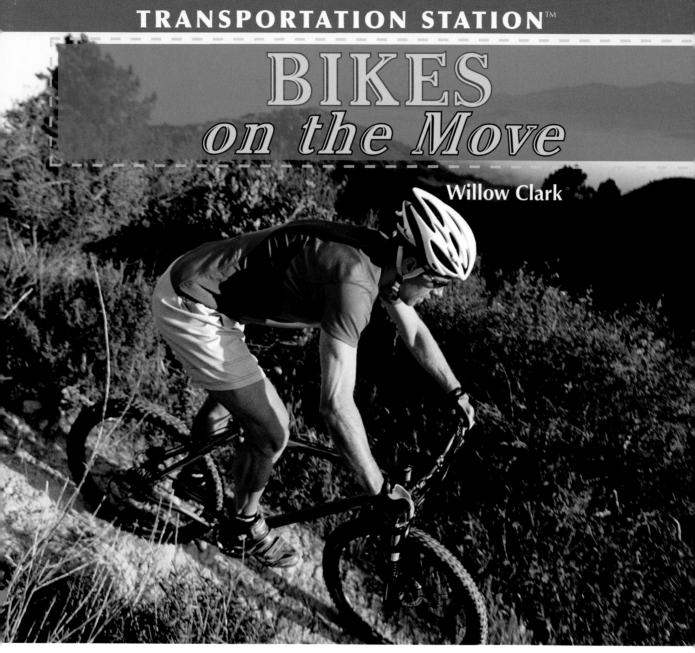

PowerKiDS
press™

New York

For Dan, riding in tandem

Published in 2010 by The Rosen Publishing Group, Inc.
29 East 21st Street, New York, NY 10010

First Edition

Editors: Nicole Pristash and Maggie Murphy
Book Design: Kate Laczynski
Photo Researcher: Jessica Gerweck

Photo Credits: Cover, p. 1 Dennis Welsh/Getty Images; pp. 4, 8, 10, 16, 20 Shutterstock. com; p. 6 Popperfoto/Getty Images; p. 12 Robert Cianflone/Getty Images; pp. 14–15 Cavan Images/Getty Images; p. 18 © Xavier Subias/agefotostock.

Library of Congress Cataloging-in-Publication Data

Clark, Willow.
  Bikes on the move / Willow Clark. — 1st ed.
      p. cm. — (Transportation station)
  Includes index.
  ISBN 978-1-4358-9334-4 (library binding) — ISBN 978-1-4358-9756-4 (pbk.) — ISBN 978-1-4358-9757-1 (6-pack)
  1. Bicycles—Juvenile literature. 2. Cycling—Juvenile literature. I. Title.
  TL412.C53 2010
  629.227'2—dc22
                                                    2009025005

Manufactured in the United States of America

CPSIA Compliance Information: Batch #WW10PK: For Further Information contact Rosen Publishing, New York, New York at 1-800-237-9932

Contents

Always remember to wear a helmet when you ride a bike, as this girl is. A helmet keeps your head safe if you fall. Helmets also come in many cool colors!

4

Let's Go for a Ride!

Have you ever taken a ride on a bicycle? Every day, millions of people all over the world ride bikes to get where they are going. Riding a bike is a lot of fun, and it is less expensive than other ways of traveling. It is also a great way to stay fit and healthy. Many people learn to ride bikes when they are young and continue to ride for years.

There are many different kinds of bikes. BMX bikes are used to race and do tricks. Mountain bikes are used to ride up steep hills and rocky mountains. Road-racing bikes are built to go fast. Do you want to know more about bikes? If so, put on your **helmet** and get ready to ride!

The size of an ordinary bicycle's front wheel depended on how tall the rider was. Some riders rode 5 feet (1.5 m) off the ground!

6

Early Bikes

The first bicycles with pedals were made in Europe during the 1860s. One type was called a boneshaker. This bike got its name because of its iron frame and wooden wheels, which made for a shaky ride on bumpy streets! Another early bike was called the ordinary bicycle. It had a giant front wheel and a small back wheel with a seat over the front tire. People often got hurt falling off of these bikes because their seats were so high off the ground.

In the 1880s, the safety bicycle was invented. This bike was easier to ride because it was lower to the ground and both of its wheels were the same size. Today's bikes are based on safety bicycles.

When riding a bike, you hold on to its handlebars, as this girl is doing. Turning the handlebars turns the front wheel. This is how you control which way you are going!

Get in Gear

Do you know how a bike works? When you push the pedals on a bike, the pedals turn a **sprocket**. The movement of the sprocket pulls a chain, which moves a gear near the rear wheel. This causes the rear wheel to turn. The movement of the rear wheel then causes the bike to move and the front wheel to turn. Now you are on your way!

Most bikes have rubber tires and frames that are made of aluminum or steel. Different bikes are built differently based on what they are used for. Racing bikes have light frames and thin tires. Mountain bikes have strong frames and thick tires. BMX bikes have small frames, but they are built to be very strong.

Mountain biking is very good exercise. Your legs work much harder when pedaling up a steep hill or mountain than when pedaling on flat ground.

Riding Off-Road

Mountain bikes are made for riding on **unpaved** roads and trails. Many people ride mountain bikes on trails where bigger vehicles, such as cars, cannot go. Mountain bikes are built to be strong so that they will not break easily. They have flat handlebars and wide tires that give the bike **traction** when going over hills and rocky areas. Some mountain bikes even have a **suspension** system, which makes the ride feel a little less bumpy.

Mountain bikes became popular in California in the 1970s. Today, there are many mountain-bike races, where riders can show off their biking skills.

BMX tricks are hard to do. It takes many years of practice to do a trick like this one! Pages 14–15: A man riding a bike down a mountain.

Races and Tricks

Have you ever heard of BMX? "BMX" stands for "bicycle **motocross**." BMX bikes are used in races and **freestyle competitions**. These bikes have smaller frames than other bikes. The seats are lower and the handlebars are higher than those on other bikes, too. BMX bikes are strong, which makes them easier to use when doing tricks and when racing.

BMX races take place on dirt tracks that often have sharp turns, hills, and jumps. In freestyle competitions, riders use BMX bikes to do tricks instead of racing against one another. When doing tricks, some riders flip their bikes high up in the air!

INFORMATION STATION

1   There are twice as many bicycles in the world as there are cars.

2   The Wright brothers, inventors of the first successful airplane, opened a bicycle shop in Ohio in 1892. It was called Wright Cycle Company.

3   Some people, such as police officers, mail carriers, and food delivery persons, use bicycles on the job.

4   Women in the 1890s generally wore long skirts. After bikes became popular, many women started to wear loose pants called bloomers, which made it easier for them to ride.

5 The greatest number of bike owners in the world live in China. There are more than 400 million bikes there!

6 A bicycle built for two or more people to ride is called a tandem bike. Like all bicycles, it has two wheels, but it has many seats and many sets of pedals.

7 Wearing a bike helmet is the best way to keep from hurting your head if you fall off your bike.

The riders shown here are racing in a 161.7-mile (260 km) road race through the city of Verase, Italy. This race was part of the 2008 World Cycling Championship.

Road-racing bikes are bikes that are built to go fast. These bikes have skinny tires and low handlebars, which help the bikes move quickly. Road-racing bikes also weigh less than other bikes weigh. Mountain bikes, for example, weigh between 25 and 35 pounds (11–16 kg). Road-racing bikes weigh around 20 pounds (9 kg).

Road-racing bikes are used in long road races, such as the Tour de France. This 2,175-mile (3,500 km) race through France and neighboring countries takes place each year. When people think of this race, they often think of rider Lance Armstrong. He has won the Tour de France seven times!

Recumbent bikes, such as this one, can often go faster than upright bicycles because they ride closer to the ground.

Lowrider bikes are just what they sound like. These bikes are built with very low seats and very high handlebars. These bikes are not made to go fast, so many people use lowriders to **cruise** the streets. Lowriders are often painted bright colors to stand out from other bikes.

A **recumbent** bike is a type of bike that has wheels that are much farther apart from each other than those on other bikes. Recumbent bikes also have seats that allow the rider to lie back while riding. People who find other bikes uncomfortable to ride may enjoy riding recumbent bikes.

These people are riding a tandem bike. In order for the bike to move correctly, the riders must pedal at the same time!

Other Cool Bikes

New ideas for bikes often come from people's biking needs. **Hybrid** bikes have features of both road-racing bikes and mountain bikes. People often use hybrid bikes to get around crowded cities because they go fast, but they can also handle the bumps and potholes of city streets.

Folding bikes have **collapsible** frames. These bikes can be broken down into one small piece. They are great for people who lack the space to store a bike. People who own folding bikes never have to search for a bike rack. They can just fold up their bike and carry it with them!

A Green Way to Ride

Bike riding is a method of transportation that does not hurt the **environment**. Unlike driving a car, biking does not produce **exhaust** that is bad for the air. Many cities are now adding bike paths so that more people will use bikes for short trips around town. Getting people to use bikes more often is a cheap and cool way for cities to do something green, or good for our Earth.

Whichever kind of bike you choose, biking will always be an exciting and easy way to travel. It is a lot of fun and a great way to see the world around you!

Glossary

collapsible (kuh-LAP-suh-bul) Can be broken down.

cruise (KROOZ) To move smoothly and easily.

environment (en-VY-ern-ment) All the living things and conditions of a place.

exhaust (ig-ZOST) Smoky air made by setting fire to gas, oil, or coal.

freestyle competitions (FREE-styl kom-peh-TIH-shunz) Events that determine the best riders in bicycle stunt riding.

helmet (HEL-mit) A covering worn to keep the head safe.

hybrid (HY-brud) A combination of different things.

motocross (MOH-toh-kros) A race on a dirt track that has sharp turns and hills.

recumbent (rih-KUM-bent) In a lying-down position.

sprocket (SPRO-ket) A wheel that has teeth, which catch on a chain to make the chain move.

suspension (suh-SPENT-shun) A shock-absorbing system.

traction (TRAK-shun) The grip a moving object has on a surface.

unpaved (UN-payvd) Not covered with something hard, such as concrete or asphalt.

Index

A
aluminum, 9

C
chain, 9

F
frame(s), 7, 9, 13, 21
freestyle competitions, 13

H
helmet, 5, 15
hills, 5, 11, 13

G
ground, 7

K
kinds, 5

L
lowriders, 19

M
motocross, 13
mountains, 5
movement, 9

P
pedals, 7, 9, 15

R
roads, 11

S
seat(s), 7, 13, 15, 19
size, 7
sprocket, 9
steel, 9
streets, 7, 19, 21
suspension, 11

T
tire(s), 7, 9, 11, 17
traction, 11
tricks, 5, 13
type, 7, 19

W
wheel(s), 7, 9, 15, 19

Web Sites

Due to the changing nature of Internet links, PowerKids Press has developed an online list of Web sites related to the subject of this book. This site is updated regularly. Please use this link to access the list: www.powerkidslinks.com/stat/bike/